WRITTEN
in my
HEART

Walks through
James Joyce's
Dublin

About the Authors

Mark Traynor is the Director of the James Joyce Centre. He coordinates the annual Bloomsday celebrations in Dublin, where he lives with his wife and daughter.

Emily Carson is a freelance writer and arts professional who has worked with the James Joyce Centre and the Bloomsday Festival. She holds an MA in French and English Literature.

About the Illustrator

Fuchsia MacAree is a freelance illustrator living and working in Dublin. She works on commercial and personal projects and also teaches illustration in the National College of Art and Design.

WRITTEN
in my
HEART

Walks through James Joyce's Dublin

MARK TRAYNOR & EMILY CARSON
ILLUSTRATED BY FUCHSIA MACAREE

THE O'BRIEN PRESS
DUBLIN

First published 2016 by The O'Brien Press Ltd,
12 Terenure Road East, Rathgar, Dublin 6, D06 HD27, Ireland.
Tel: +353 1 4923333; Fax: +353 1 4922777
E-mail: books@obrien.ie
Website: www.obrien.ie
The O'Brien Press is a member of Publishing Ireland.

in association with

The James Joyce Centre,
35 North Great George's Street, Dublin 1, D01 WK44, Ireland.
Tel: +353 1 8788547
Email: info@jamesjoyce.ie
Website: www.jamesjoyce.ie

ISBN: 978-1-84717-820-6

1 3 5 7 8 6 4 2
16 18 20 19 17

Printed and bound in Poland by Białostockie Zakłady Graficzne S.A.
The paper in this book is produced using pulp from managed forests.

Published in

DUBLIN

UNESCO
City of Literature

WRITTEN in my HEART

Walks through James Joyce's Dublin

Foreword

Joyce and Dublin are inextricably linked. Mention our city in London, Paris or New York, and often people will murmur *James Joyce*. He himself said that when he was dead, Dublin would be found written in his heart. He played games with visitors to his Paris flat, challenging them to name the shops and buildings on O'Connell Street – and he invariably won. In the 1930s, when someone asked him when he would return to Dublin, he replied, 'Have I ever left it?' But although he famously remarked that if Dublin were destroyed, it could be rebuilt from the pages of *Ulysses*, this is not strictly true. What he has left us with is, in fact, a very detailed and accurate street map of Dublin, but with little description of the external fabric.

This is the kind of little book that, in other circumstances, might have found its way into Mr. Leopold Bloom's pocket. It is a companionable guide to the Dublin of James Joyce and his family. I myself started doing walking tours some forty years ago with international postgraduate students from Trinity College. This was taken over and made his own by Joyce's nephew, the late Ken Monaghan. Walking tours form a significant part of the facilities offered by the James Joyce Centre in North Great George's Street. Take this little book with you and enjoy what remains of the Dublin of James Joyce.

Senator David Norris,
Dublin

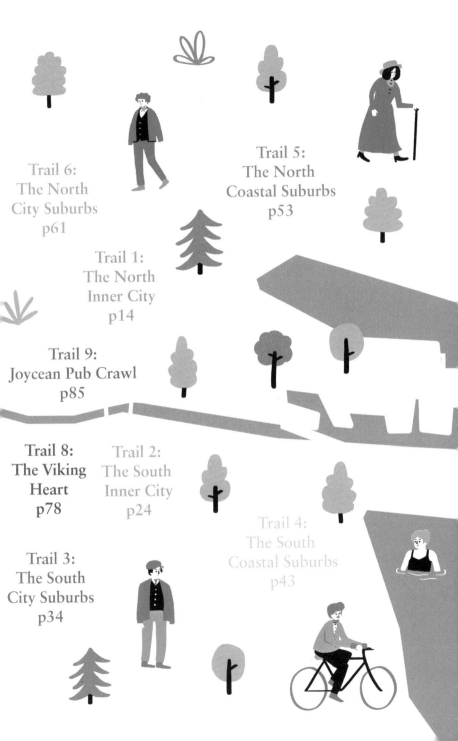

Introduction

On the 10th of June, 1927, James Joyce visited the Tsar Peter House in the city of Zaandam in the Netherlands. There he signed his name in the visitors' book, listing his place of residence as 'Dublin'. Given that Joyce had left Ireland more or less for good in 1904 at the age of twenty-two, this might seem somewhat unusual. But as you will discover in these pages, the author's relationship with this city was a turbulent and complex one. His father, John Stanislaus Joyce, quipped upon learning of James's relationship with Nora Barnacle, 'she'll always stick to him'; in the same way, we might also say that despite the time and distance Joyce spent away from Dublin, the city always stuck to him, and he to it.

We have to reach for a German rather than an English dictionary to find a word that concisely describes this bond: *Hassliebe*, an amalgam of hate (*Hass*) and love (*Liebe*). It is certainly the case that while Joyce displayed frustration and occasional contempt for his hometown, his words and remarks equally betray an almost mystical attraction to and obsession with the city that made him. He was, he once remarked, 'attached to it daily and nightly like an umbilical cord'. All of his major works are set in Dublin, and all deploy such an exacting picture of the topography, history and culture of the city that Joyce and his birthplace have become indelibly ingrained in each other's myths.

It is also important to understand that James Joyce maintained deep familial associations with the city. As we shall see, the political and social history of Dublin depicted in his works is often viewed through the prism of the Joyce family narrative. Expressing his guilt at not having returned home to attend his father's funeral in 1932, for instance, he remarked in a letter to Harriet Shaw Weaver:

> *Why go on writing about a place I did not dare to go*
> *to at such a moment, where not three persons know me*
> *or understand me? . . . Hundreds of pages and scores*
> *of characters in my books came from [my father].*

In part, it is possible to trace the growth and decline of the Joyce family by way of their peregrinations across the city. James, the eldest child, was born on the 2nd of February, 1882, at 41 Brighton Square in Rathgar, and his early years were marked by middle-class comfort. As the family grew, they moved to larger homes in the affluent south and coastal suburbs. Their eventual journey north across the Liffey marks the beginning of their decline, as the alcoholic and profligate John Joyce plunged them into very real poverty. The family's movements and the grand sweep of their fortunes are mirrored in Joyce's work, particularly his first novel, *A Portrait of the Artist as a Young Man*, and it remains a narrative written into the fabric of the streets and buildings of the city. While not exhaustive, this book offers itself as a starting point for those who wish to get a sense of how the history of the Joyces is also inscribed into the geography of Dublin.

Across the span of Joyce's work, from the coiled minimalism of *Dubliners* to the final wordy eruption of *Finnegans Wake*, the city is mapped out in a manner that is as sublime and grotesque as it is unforgettable. Who else could grasp the quality of the Irish Sea as Joyce does in the opening passages of *Ulysses*: 'The snotgreen sea. The scrotumtightening sea.' As you stand atop the Martello Tower in Sandycove today, watching the swimmers bobbing in the tide at the Forty Foot, these words perfectly capture the character of the bay before you.

Of course, another aim of this book is to demonstrate just how deeply embedded the geography of the city is in Joyce's work. The Russian novelist Vladimir Nabokov insisted that teachers of *Ulysses* prepare their students first with maps of Dublin:

> *Instead of perpetuating the pretentious nonsense of Homeric, chromatic and visceral chapter headings, instructors should prepare maps of Dublin with Bloom's and Stephen's intertwining itineraries clearly traced.*

While *Dubliners* and *A Portrait...* offer the odd sumptuous detail about areas of the city, readers of Joyce might be forgiven for feeling disoriented in his dizzying depictions of Dublin; nowhere more so than in the seemingly volatile, abrupt episodes of *Ulysses* and the dark labyrinth of *Finnegans Wake*. As Joyce's confidant Frank Budgen wrote:

It is not by way of description that Dublin is created in Ulysses. *There is a wealth of delicate pictorial evidence in* Dubliners, *but there is little or none in* Ulysses. *Streets are named but never described.*

We hope the trails contained in this book illuminate some of the denser allusions to the streets, houses, churches and pubs that echo through the work.

When asked whether or not he had read all of *Ulysses*, the late, great Argentine author Jorge Luis Borges replied that while he had not, he nevertheless knew what it was, just as one can know a city without having explored all of its streets. This little book takes an equally humble approach to Joyce's Dublin. The trails herein are not an all-encompassing survey of every street and lane, but rather a starting point for seeing the city through the unique lens of Joyce, both the young man who lived there and the artist who forged it in his imagination. Joyce told his friend Arthur Power:

For myself, I always write about Dublin, because if I can get to the heart of Dublin I can get to the heart of all the cities of the world.

We hope that, armed with his books and this guide, you might begin your own journey into the heart of Joyce's Dublin.

Mark Traynor,
Director of the James Joyce Centre, Dublin

The North Inner City

Dublin was a new and complex sensation...

We begin our journey in the heart of north Dublin city, a
focal point for much of Joyce's work. It was in this area that
Joyce spent his formative years, attending school at Belvedere
College and exploring the streets on long, circuitous walks.

This trail examines a time when Joyce's family was descending
into poverty, with father John Joyce's career as a rates
collector thrown into doubt, and his propensity for drinking
and reckless spending on the rise.

The stops on this trail also display the decline of north
inner-city Dublin that began in the early 1800s. We'll take in
everything from the once opulent and highly prized Georgian
houses of Mountjoy Square to the decrepit site of Dublin's
infamous red-light district.

1 The James Joyce Centre, 35 North Great George's St.

Our tour begins at the heart of Joycean activity in the city, the James Joyce Centre. Number 35 was built in 1784 for Valentine Brown, the Earl of Kenmare, who used it as his townhouse. The interior plasterwork is by Michael Stapleton, one of the finest stuccodores of the time, whose work also adorns nearby Belvedere College.

Although Joyce never lived in this house, he had a connection with it through Professor Denis J. Maginni, who ran a dance academy here. Maginni appears several times in *Ulysses*. In the 'Wandering Rocks' episode, he is described as wearing a 'silk hat, slate frockcoat with silk facings, white kerchief tie, tight lavender trousers, canary gloves and pointed patent boots'.

Within the Centre, you'll find exhibitions about Joyce's life and work as well as stunning décor and the front door of 7 Eccles Street, home to the Bloom family in *Ulysses*.

2 Belvedere College, 6 Great Denmark St.

Directly up the street from the James Joyce Centre sits Belvedere College, one of Joyce's *almae matres* and the backdrop for much of *A Portrait of the Artist as a Young Man*. Built in 1832, the school is run by the Jesuit order (as was Joyce's previous school, Clongowes Wood in Kildare). His descriptions through the eyes of Stephen Dedalus paint a picture of a disciplined but tolerant schooling experience:

His masters, even when they had not attracted him, had seemed to him always intelligent and serious priests, athletic and high-spirited prefects. He thought of them as men who washed their bodies briskly with cold water and wore clean cold linen.

One person who surely had an impact on Joyce's writing was his English and geography teacher, Mr. Dempsey. It was he who introduced the student to *The Adventures of Ulysses* by Charles Lamb, which would influence his greatest novel.

3 Hardwicke St.

This street represents the first inner-city address of the Joyces, who had been ousted from their home in the leafy, affluent suburb of Blackrock. They lived briefly in number 29, and although the original building was demolished in 1954, the homes at the North Frederick Street end are reminiscent of the type of house the Joyces lived in. The family's move had quite an effect on young James, as described in *A Portrait…*:

… the sudden flight from the comfort and revery of Blackrock, the passage through the gloomy foggy city, the thought of the bare cheerless house in which they were now to live made his heart heavy …

Hardwicke Street is also the setting for 'The Boarding House' in *Dubliners*, in which the madam of the house, Mrs. Mooney, plots to marry off her daughter Polly ('a little perverse Madonna') to one of her naïve young boarders, Mr. Doran.

④ 7 Eccles St.

Number 7 is best known as the home of *Ulysses* protagonist Leopold Bloom, but Joyce had some experience with the address too. His friend J. F. Byrne was living there in 1909 when Joyce returned from Trieste with his son Giorgio. It was during this visit that Joyce, having been misinformed about his partner Nora's romantic past, fired off accusatory letters to her in Trieste. Byrne eventually calmed him down, convincing him of her loyalty. Unsurprising, then, that the home of the Blooms is also one in which infidelity, jealousy and suspicion are at play.

The house would have been on the site of the now expanded Mater Misericordiae Hospital. Much of the 'Calypso' episode of *Ulysses* takes place here. Leopold Bloom prepares an unusual breakfast of fried kidneys and tea, and Joyce gives us a detailed play-by-play of his bowel movements!

⑤ St Francis Xavier Church, Upper Gardiner St.

This Catholic church sits proudly at the top of Gardiner Street, with imposing Ionic pillars and golden Latin script. Also known as Gardiner Street Church, it features in the *Dubliners* story 'Grace'. When Mr. Kernan falls down a flight of stairs and bites off part of his tongue after too many drinks, his friends stage

18

an intervention and send him on a retreat that begins here:

The transept of the Jesuit Church in Gardiner Street was almost full ... The light of the lamps of the church fell upon an assembly of black clothes and white collars, relieved here and there by tweeds, on dark mottled pillars of green marble and on lugubrious canvases.

This episode was based on John Joyce's own retreat with a few friends to remedy his drinking problem. Stanislaus Joyce wrote about it in his diary, which his brother James dipped into as source material.

6 Mountjoy Square

This Georgian square, one of five in Dublin, has been a stomping ground for many Irish literary figures since its construction in the 18th Century. While Joyce lived nearby, W.B. Yeats spent a great deal of time at number 53 and Sean O'Casey lived on the square itself. O'Casey, a resident of number 35, even set his play *The Shadow of a Gunman* at this address.

In the 'Wandering Rocks' episode of *Ulysses*, Father John Conmee crosses the east of the square on his way to Fairview. Father Conmee was an important figure from Joyce's schooldays. Having been rector at Clongowes Wood, Joyce's first school, he then moved to Belvedere College. A fortuitous meeting with Joyce's father in 1893 at the corner of Mountjoy Square led to James and his brother Stanislaus being enrolled in Belvedere with their fees waived. In *A Portrait...* he's described as 'the decentest rector that ever was in Clongowes'.

7 14 (now 34) Fitzgibbon St.

Not far from Mountjoy Square is number 14 (now 34) Fitzgibbon Street, a large Georgian house that is considered to be the Joyces' last 'respectable' address.

The family lived here for about a year, during which time John Joyce had his serendipitous encounter with Father Conmee. Before moving on to Belvedere, for several months James and Stanislaus were enrolled at the nearby O'Connell School, a situation their father was not happy about. Joyce writes about this in *A Portrait…*:

'Christian brothers bedamned!' said Mr. Dedalus. 'Is it with Paddy Stink and Mickey Mud? No, let him stick to the jesuits in God's name since he began with them.'

8 13 North Richmond St.

Number 13 was the last of the Joyces' inner-city addresses; the family would move towards the northern suburbs as they fell deeper into poverty. Joyce lived here for only three years, but his biographer Richard Ellmann argues that this street yielded more characters and references in his work than any other in Dublin.

North Richmond Street features in 'An Encounter', 'Araby' and 'The Sisters' in *Dubliners*, and characters from five of its twenty houses appear in *Dubliners*, *Finnegans Wake* and, most extensively, *Ulysses*. The story 'Araby' begins thus:

North Richmond Street, being blind, was a quiet street except at the hour when the Christian Brothers' School set the boys free. An uninhabited house of two storeys stood at the blind end, detached from its neighbours in a square ground. The other houses of the street, conscious of decent lives within them, gazed at one another with brown imperturbable faces.

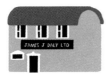

9 Railway St.

This street seems almost forgotten today, lined as it is with derelict buildings and dreary apartment blocks, yet this was once the beating heart of what was purported to be Europe's largest red-light district: Monto. It is said that Joyce began to frequent brothels in Monto at the tender age of fourteen, and he later set an entire episode of *Ulysses* here.

'Circe' follows Leopold Bloom and Stephen Dedalus as they delve into Dublin's seedy underbelly, nighttown, engaging with local prostitutes as they experience intense hallucinations. Joyce paints a vivid picture of the dark and gloomy surroundings:

The Mabbot Street entrance of nighttown, before which stretches an uncobbled tramsiding set with skeleton tracks, red and green will-o'-the-wisps and danger signals. Rows of grimy houses with gaping doors.

If you walk around the corner to number 7–8 Beaver Street, you will find a disused brush factory (with the sign 'James J Daly Ltd') which was the location of one of the last brothels in the area.

21

throughout the author's work.

In Joyce's time, this was officially called Sackville Street but commonly referred to as O'Connell Street after the statue of Daniel O'Connell was unveiled at the far end in the year of Joyce's birth. It pops up a few times in *Finnegans Wake*, described as 'Shackvulle Strutt' and 'Lower O'Connell Street ... Laura Connor's treat'.

10 The Parnell Monument, top of O'Connell St.

Returning west by Sean MacDermott Street and Cathal Brugha Street, you reach the top of Dublin's largest thoroughfare. There you are greeted by the monument of Charles Stewart Parnell. Erected in 1911, this is one of the statues on O'Connell Street that Joyce wouldn't have seen day to day while he lived in Dublin. This is unfortunate, as Parnell was responsible for Joyce's first foray into writing; his death inspired the nine-year-old Joyce to write a poem called 'Et Tu, Healy', and he remained a figure of interest

11 GPO & site of Nelson's Pillar, middle O'Connell St.

As you walk down O'Connell Street, passing by the Gresham Hotel (see Trail 9), there are two attractions worth noting: the General Post Office, the temporary HQ of the Irish rebels during the 1916 Rising and the oldest functioning post office in the world (since 1818);

and the gigantic Spire, the erstwhile location of Nelson's Pillar, which was bombed by Republican activists in 1966. The pillar features in Stephen Dedalus' Parable of the Plums in the 'Aeolus' episode of *Ulysses*.

In the early 20th Century, O'Connell Street was nicknamed 'the street of the three adulterers' after the men featured in its main statues: Parnell, who fell for the married Katherine O'Shea; Lord Horatio Nelson, who similarly fell for Lady Emma Hamilton; and O'Connell, who had a rumoured weakness for illicit affairs. W.B. Yeats remarked in a Seanad debate in 1925, 'It was said about O'Connell, in his own day, that you could not throw a stick over a workhouse wall without hitting one of his children.'

Did You Know?

Until October 1916, Ireland existed in a different time zone to the rest of Great Britain. Known as 'Dublin Mean Time' or 'Dunsink Mean Time', it ran 25 minutes and 21 seconds behind Greenwich Mean Time. The time zone was established in 1880 with the Definition of Time Act, taking its coordinates from the Dunsink Observatory in Castleknock. A small number of time keeps in the city kept Imperial time, such as the time-ball on the Ballast Office, which dropped at one o'clock Greenwich time each day. Early in the 'Lestrygonians' episode of *Ulysses*, Bloom thinks that it is past one o'clock because the time-ball is down. It is only later that he realises he has been crossing the city in the wrong time zone!

RIVER LIFFEY
SOUTH QUAYS
Temple Bar
Trinity College
PEARSE ST
DAME ST
DART
NASSAU ST
GEORGE'S ST
GRAFTON ST
AUNGIER ST
MOUNT ST LOWER
Merrion Square
MOUNT ST UPPER
Stephen's Green
CUFFE ST
BAGGOT ST
1
2
3
4
5
6
7
8
9
10
11
12

TRAIL 2:

The South Inner City

*Mr. Bloom, quickbreathing, slowlier
walking passed Adam court.*

As we move across the Liffey, we hit another area that plays
a recurring role in Joyce's works. The south city provided the
backdrop for his late teens and early twenties, when Joyce
was studying in University College Dublin on Stephen's Green.
Many of the spots on this trail had a huge influence on his life,
be it literary or personal. It was here that he first met his wife-
to-be, Nora Barnacle, and the inimitable W.B. Yeats.

This part of the city is the focal point of the 'Lestrygonians'
episode of *Ulysses*, where Leopold Bloom's thoughts flit from
topic to topic as he considers his lunch.

We begin on Westmoreland Street, the gateway to the south city
from the River Liffey.

① Westmoreland St.

This thoroughfare runs from O'Connell Bridge towards College Green. It is described vividly in the *Dubliners* story 'Counterparts':

In Westmoreland Street the footpaths were crowded with young men and women returning from business and ragged urchins ran here and there yelling out the names of evening editions.

In *Ulysses*, Bloom walks down Westmoreland Street on his way to get lunch in the 'Lestrygonians' episode. He is stopped by a former flame, Josie Breen, outside number 29. Today, you can see here one of the fourteen bronze plaques that chart Bloom's trail across the city. In this episode, his mind is consumed by thoughts of food. Number 29 would once have been Harrison's, where Bloom dreams of 'hot mockturtle vapour and steam of newbaked jampuffs rolypoly'.

② Dame St.

This commercial street stretches from Trinity College to City Hall. In the *Dubliners* story 'Two Gallants', the sleazy Corley picks up a woman here:

'One night, man,' he said, 'I was going along Dame Street and I spotted a fine tart under Waterhouse's clock and said good-night you know. So we went for a walk round by the canal and she told me she was a slavey in a house in Baggot Street, I put my arm round her and squeezed her a bit that night.'

The great, hulking Central Bank, on the edge of Temple Bar, was once the site of Jury's Hotel, which is mentioned in the 'Cyclops' episode of *Ulysses*. Jury's was demolished in the 1970s, but a group of Swiss businessmen bought its beautiful antique bar and shipped it, in its entirety, to Zurich, where it is now at the heart of the James Joyce Pub.

③ Grafton St.

It may seem hard to believe now, but Grafton Street was developed from a country lane in 1708 in honour of Henry FitzRoy, the 1st Duke of Grafton. Originally an upmarket residential street, Grafton Street became a main city thoroughfare after the erection of O'Connell Bridge. By the turn of the 20th Century, it was the top shopping street in the city.

In 1849 Brown Thomas was opened by the drapers Hugh Brown and James Thomas, and it would later become Ireland's most prestigious department store. In 'Lestrygonians', Bloom makes his way up Grafton Street and lingers in front of the shop's hallowed windows (at that time located across the street, where Marks & Spencer now resides), full of the styles of the era:

He passed, dallying, the windows of Brown Thomas, silk mercers. Cascades of ribbons. Flimsy China silks ... Gleaming silks, petticoats on slim brass rails, rays of flat silk stockings.

4 85–86 St. Stephen's Green

Stephen's Green was the original home of University College Dublin, where Joyce studied modern languages. In *A Portrait...*, Stephen crosses the green each morning on his way to the university's fine Georgian townhouses:

But the trees in Stephen's Green were fragrant of rain and the rain-sodden earth gave its mortal odour, a faint incense rising upward through the mould of many hearts.

Number 86 was founded as a Catholic university by John Henry Newman in 1854. The university later expanded into number 85, and in addition to Joyce boasts an impressive alumni including the poet Gerard Manley Hopkins and revolutionary Patrick Pearse. Joyce studied Latin, French, English, Mathematics and Philosophy in his first year. The buildings are now known as Newman House and, although they are currently undergoing major renovations, the stunning interiors feature elaborate period plasterwork and are worth visiting when the site reopens in 2018.

5 Kildare St.

It was on Kildare Street, near the National Library, that Joyce met W.B. Yeats for the first time in October 1902. The young Joyce was introduced to Yeats by the poet George William Russell (Æ). Yeats was rarely in Dublin but had returned to help with a staging of *Cathleen Ni Houlihan* in the Antient Concert Rooms on Pearse Street. Joyce took his chance to have a face-to-face discussion with the revered poet.

When they met, Joyce read some of his own poetry and then dismissed the favourable feedback that Yeats gave him, saying they would both 'soon be forgotten'. As a parting shot, Joyce is supposed to have told Yeats he was 'too old to be helped' – something Yeats probably wasn't counting on in a meeting with a young, unknown writer.

6 National Maternity Hospital, Holles St.

Pregnancy plays a recurring part in *Ulysses*, and one episode, 'Oxen of the Sun', takes place in the National Maternity Hospital just off Merrion Square. It is here that Mina Purefoy experiences a long and difficult labour while Bloom and a group of doctors gather in the common room to drink beer, eat sardines and discuss philosophical matters.

The nursing woman answered him and said that that woman was in throes now full three days and that it would be a hard birth unneth to bear but that now in a little it would be. She said thereto that she had seen many births of women but never was none so hard as was that woman's birth.

7 Antient Concert Rooms, 52 Great Brunswick St. (now Pearse St.)

This was one of the most popular venues in the city in Joyce's time; he himself even performed there several times. A talented singer, Joyce sang at the annual Feis Ceoil in 1904 and was about to be awarded first prize when he refused to do a sight reading of a piece and stormed off stage. As a result he was awarded a bronze medal, which today is owned by former *Riverdance* star Michael Flatley.

In Joyce's own work, the Antient Concert Rooms provide the setting for 'A Mother' in *Dubliners*, in which Mrs. Kearney splashes out when her daughter has her big debut as an accompanist at a series of concerts:

Everything went on smoothly. Mrs. Kearney bought some lovely blush-pink charmeuse in Brown Thomas's to let into the front of Kathleen's dress. It cost a pretty penny; but there are occasions when a little expense is justifiable.

8 Sweny's Pharmacy, Lincoln Place

Sweny's has barely changed since Joyce's time. You can still purchase a 'cake of new clean lemon soap' like the one that Bloom procures in the 'Lotus Eaters' episode of *Ulysses*:

Mr Bloom raised a cake to his nostrils. Sweet lemony wax.
— I'll take this one, he said.

Sweny's remains one of the most colourful Joycean landmarks in the city. It is often described as having been 'preserved through neglect', in that no moves were ever made to modernise it. Nowadays you're better off attending the pharmacy for one of its readings than to try to buy medicines – although unopened medical jars and uncollected prescriptions still sit in their cabinets!

⑨ Merrion Square

Number 1 Merrion Square was the proposed meeting place for James Joyce and Nora Barnacle's first date on the 14th of June, 1904. It was well known to Dubliners as the home of Sir William Wilde (whose son Oscar is the subject of some banter in *Ulysses*) and is now part of the American College Dublin. Nora was unable to get time off

work to come and meet him at Merrion Square, so they resolved to meet a couple of days later on the 16th – the date that Joyce later immortalised in *Ulysses*.

Joyce's contemporaries George William Russell (Æ) and W.B. Yeats both held addresses at Merrion Square, as did an important influence, Joseph Sheridan Le Fanu. Today, Le Fanu's residence is home to the Irish Arts Council.

⑩ National Library of Ireland, Kildare St.

The National Library is the setting for the 'Scylla and Charybdis' episode of *Ulysses*, where Stephen Dedalus presents his *Hamlet* theory to real-life Irish Literary Revival figures John Eglinton, Æ and Thomas Lyster.

Established in 1877, the National Library now houses an impressive collection of Joyce's personal notes and literary papers. These include letters between Joyce and his close friend Paul Léon, with whom he consulted in Paris while writing *Finnegans Wake*. Léon was so embroiled in Joyce's affairs that he acted as his secretary, agent and legal advisor, and the letters give a fascinating insight into the writer's business dealings at that time. The library is also home to The Joyce Papers 2002, which include some of the earliest drafts of many of the episodes in *Ulysses*.

11 Freemasons' Hall, 17 Molesworth St.

This Grand Lodge of Ireland makes an appearance in *Ulysses*, and there are many masonic references peppering Joyce's works. In the 'Lestrygonians' episode of *Ulysses*, Bloom helps a young blind boy across Dawson Street before passing the Freemasons' Hall, remarking:

Sir Frederick Falkiner going into the freemasons' hall. Solemn as Troy.

Throughout the book, many characters make reference to freemasons and masonic lodges. Joyce wrote to his close friend Frank Budgen in 1921 in search of a handbook on freemasonry, presumably for research.

The Molesworth Street lodge is the oldest in continuous existence in the world. Today the lodge is largely open to the public, with tours available in the summer months – just in case you want to find out what interested Joyce so much about this secretive order!

12 Nassau St.

This is where Joyce first met his wife-to-be Nora Barnacle on Friday, the 10th of June, 1904. It is said that he spotted Nora on the street and struck up a conversation with her, then they hastily made a date to meet again on the 14th of June.

Nora was working as a chambermaid in the nearby Finn's Hotel, whose sign is still visible over the railings of Trinity College. She mistook Joyce for a Swedish sailor, with his blue eyes and yachting cap. He began referring to her in letters shortly afterwards as 'particularly pouting Nora'.

When Joyce's father heard Nora's name, he purportedly joked that she would 'never leave him', in the same way that a barnacle attaches itself to a ship for life.

Did You Know?

Although Joyce's first encounter with W.B. Yeats didn't get off to a flying start, Yeats became one of Joyce's earliest supporters. As an established writer, the older poet did a great deal to assist Joyce with contacts and advice; for instance, he backed Joyce's application for the Royal Literary Fund in 1915. When Yeats set about establishing an Irish Academy in the late 1930s, he invited the younger man to join, although Joyce declined. It is reported that following the death of Yeats, Joyce conceded that he felt Yeats was a greater writer than him.

CAMDEN ST

HARCOURT RD

SOUTH CIRCULAR RD

Portobello

GRAND CANAL

GROVE RD

RATHGAR

MILITARY RD

Rathmines

CASTLEWOOD AVE

Rathgar

RATHMINES ROAD

Terenure

The South City Suburbs

*Once upon a time and a very good time it was there
was a moocow coming down along the road and
this moocow that was coming down along the road
met a nicens little boy named baby tuckoo.*

This trail will take us out of Dublin's inner city and into the
southern suburbs of Portobello, Rathmines, Rathgar and
Terenure. Here we'll find the birthplace not only of *Ulysses*
protagonist Leopold Bloom but also of Joyce himself.

Joyce's parents spent a lot of time in these areas, and Joyce
frequented the house of George 'Æ' Russell in Portobello to
help develop his literary style. This part of Dublin also has
links to the Irish Jewish community, a small but influential
group at the time.

Our tour begins in Portobello, the heart of Jewish Dublin, and
finishes near Joyce's first home in Rathgar.

1 52 Clanbrassil St. Upper

In *Ulysses*, Joyce gives this as the address of Rudolph Virag, a Hungarian Jew from Szombathely who immigrated to Ireland, converted from Judaism to Protestantism, and changed his name to Rudolph Bloom. Although Joyce doesn't stipulate whether the house is on Clanbrassil Street Upper or Lower, a plaque was erected here to mark the birth of Rudolph's son Leopold in May 1866.

One of the few protagonists in modern literature to be honoured with his own annual celebration in Bloomsday, Leopold Bloom was born and raised in the heart of what was then called 'Little Jerusalem'. In the year of his birth, the number of Jews in Ireland would have been around 200; by 1904, this would have been closer to 5,000. Today, these numbers have dwindled to around 2,000. The Jewish community in Portobello would have grown rapidly during the time Joyce lived in Dublin.

2 33 Emorville Avenue

Nearby, along the winding streets of Portobello, is the home of George William Russell, the Irish writer, poet, artist and critic who wrote under the pseudonym Æ. He was introduced to Joyce in 1902 and features prominently in the 'Scylla and Charybdis' episode in *Ulysses*. He is credited with having introduced Joyce to many Irish literary figures, including W.B. Yeats and Lady Gregory.

Russell was involved with Irish nationalism and the Theosophical movement; as the poet Æ, he also claimed to be a clairvoyant who could make contact with spiritual beings, and this was the subject matter for much of his work.

Russell once wrote of Joyce:

There is a young boy named Joyce who may do something. He is proud as Lucifer and writes verses perfect in their technique and sometimes beautiful in quality.

3 33 Synge St.

Portobello is also the birthplace of Irish playwright George Bernard Shaw, who was born at 33 Synge Street in 1856. Shaw is most notable for his considerable number of plays – he wrote more than sixty over his lifetime – and for being the only person ever to have received both a Nobel Prize for Literature and an Oscar.

In 1921, Joyce's agent, Sylvia Beach, asked Shaw to subscribe in advance to the first publication of *Ulysses*. Shaw refused, saying that he had read parts of the book in serial format and found Joyce's depiction of Dublin to be 'hardly bearable':

I could not write the words Mr. Joyce uses: my prudish hand would refuse to form the letters; and I can find no interest in his infantile clinical incontinences, or in the flatulations which he thinks worth mentioning ...

4 The Irish Jewish Museum, 3 Walworth Road

The erstwhile Walworth Road Synagogue is now home to the Irish Jewish Museum. Jewish people began to settle in this area of Dublin in the 1870s, many having fled Eastern Europe due to Russian persecution.

In January 1904, as a result of the 'Limerick Pogrom', many Jewish people in the west of Ireland were driven from their homes. Having set *Ulysses* in 1904, Joyce would have been aware of this event. This is perhaps reflected in the anti-Semitic sentiment that pervades the book, such as when Stephen's employer Mr. Deasy incorrectly boasts that Ireland is the only country never to have persecuted the Jews 'because she never let them in'.

These tensions come to a head in the 'Cyclops' episode, wherein the Citizen, an aggressive Republican, vents his anti-Semitic venom upon Bloom, who responds:

'I belong to a race too,' says Bloom, 'that is hated and persecuted. Also now. This very moment. This very instant.'

5 Portobello Bridge

Officially called La Touche Bridge, this marks the move from Dublin city centre to the suburb of Rathmines. It was the scene of the arrest of one of Joyce's closest university friends, Francis Sheehy-Skeffington. The pair co-published a pamphlet in 1901 – Joyce's first piece of published material – and Sheehy-Skeffington appears in *A Portrait of the Artist as a Young Man* as the character McCann.

During the Easter Rising of 1916, Sheehy-Skeffington, a pacifist, called a meeting in the city centre to gather support for a civilian taskforce to combat looting. On his way home, he was stopped on Portobello Bridge and arrested, though no charge was given. He was taken to nearby Cathal Brugha Barracks in Rathmines and shot by firing squad the next day.

6 Rathmines Road

As we make our way towards the bustling suburb of Rathmines, we pass along what used to be one of the main transport routes into the city centre. In 1872, a horse-drawn tram service began operating between College Green and Rathgar, followed by other suburban routes over the next decade. References to the trams and their stops are peppered throughout *Ulysses*, so much so that there has even been a book published on the subject: *The Bloomsday Trams* by David Foley.

In *Ulysses*, at the beginning of 'Aeolus', we get a sense of all these routes:

In the heart of the Hibernian metropolis. Before Nelson's pillar trams slowed, shunted, changed trolley, started for Blackrock, Kingstown and Dalkey, Clonskea, Rathgar and Terenure, Palmerston Park and upper Rathmines, Sandymount Green, Rathmines, Ringsend and Sandymount Tower, Harold's Cross. The hoarse Dublin United Tramway Company's timekeeper bawled them off …

7 Rathmines Catholic Church

The beautiful Church of Mary Immaculate, Refuge of Sinners, originated in 1830 and is something of a landmark, its distinctive copper dome visible from the city centre. In *Ulysses* it is spied from atop Nelson's Pillar on Sackville (O'Connell) Street: 'They see the roofs and argue about what the different churches are: Rathmines' blue dome, Adam and Eve's, saint Laurence O'Toole's.'

It is said that the dome was in fact originally bound for St. Petersburg but was diverted to Dublin because of the social and political upheaval in Russia. Joyce's parents married here on the 5th of May, 1880, when May Murray was twenty years old and John Joyce was thirty.

8 23 Castlewood Avenue

Turning from the main thoroughfare of Rathmines Road, we take a quick detour onto Castlewood Avenue. The Joyces lived at this address from 1884, and as it was a more spacious residence than their previous one on Brighton Square, it allowed the family to grow. Three Joyce sons (including Stanislaus, James's closest sibling) were born in the three years the family

lived here, joining James and Poppie, who had entered the world up the road in Rathgar.

Today, this lovely Victorian house bears a plaque referring to Joyce's time there; it has hardly changed from how it would have looked in his day.

9 The Church of the Three Patrons, Rathgar Road

Diverging from Rathmines, we now start walking towards Joyce's birthplace, along Rathgar Road. The Church of the Three Patrons sits at the centre of the road, a plain, hulking edifice that was built between 1860 and 1862 by Patrick Byrne, the same architect who designed Rathmines Catholic Church.

This was popularly known as 'the servants' church' because in the late 19th and early 20th centuries it was the main place

⑩ 41 Brighton Square, Rathgar

Taking a short detour from Rathgar Road, we hit the unusually named Brighton Square, which is really more of a triangle. Number 41 is the birthplace of James Augustus Joyce, on the 2nd of February, 1882. It was also the birthplace of his sister Margaret 'Poppie' Joyce in 1884. Brighton Square features in the opening of *A Portrait...* as a reference to a story Joyce's father had told him as a child. John Joyce wrote to his son in later life:

I wonder do you recollect the old days in Brighton Square, when you were Babie Tuckoo, and I used to take you out in the Square and tell you all about the moo-cow that used to come down from the mountain and take little boys across?

Although Joyce would have had no recollection of Brighton Square, minor allusions are made to it in his work. In *Ulysses*, Molly Bloom lives on Brighton Square before she marries Leopold, and in her final soliloquy, she makes reference to how Leopold had almost proposed to her there as she made potato cakes.

of worship for the servants who worked and lived in the large houses in the area.

John Joyce and May Murray sang together in a choir here; it was said to be among the finest in Dublin at the time. In *Ulysses,* we learn that Stephen Dedalus was baptised here, and it was one of the three places in which Leopold Bloom was baptised.

11 Terenure village

Just round the corner from Brighton Square is Terenure village. Formerly known as Roundtown, in Joyce's time the village was the terminus point for numerous trams at its main crossroads. It features in a lovely, descriptive paragraph about playing boules in the 'Oxen of the Sun' episode of *Ulysses:*

*A shaven space of lawn
one soft May evening, the
wellremembered grove of lilacs*

*at Roundtown, purple and white,
fragrant slender spectators of
the game but with much real
interest in the pellets as they run
slowly forward over the sward
or collide and stop, one by its
fellow, with a brief alert shock.*

The pub at the crossroads, Vaughan's Eagle House, was the rather less grand birthplace of Joyce's mother, May Murray, whose father was the owner.

12 St. Joseph's Church

Turning back towards the city centre, we hit the final stop on this trail. St. Joseph's Catholic Church contains a window by Harry Clarke – one of Ireland's most celebrated stained-glass artists – and it was on this site that James Joyce was baptised in 1882.

The South Coastal Suburbs

Stately, plump Buck Mulligan came from the stairhead, bearing a bowl of lather on which a mirror and a razor lay crossed.

Dublin's south coastal suburbs stretch over 20km from Ringsend, near Dublin Port, out toward the picturesque villages of Sandycove and Dalkey. The Joyce family lived in several addresses dotted along Dublin's coastline, and their northward trail of migration from Bray, County Wicklow, towards the city centre and the north coastal suburbs outlined the family's declining fortunes.

This trail also features a few of the homes in which Joyce lived briefly during adulthood. He continued to move from house to house as he raised his own family, across cities such as Pula, Trieste, Rome, Zurich and Paris.

This trail is best followed by taking the Dublin commuter rail (the DART) southbound from the city centre. Alighting at Grand Canal Dock, Blackrock, Sandycove and Bray will allow you to follow in the footsteps of both Joyce and his characters, while taking in the beauty of Dublin Bay.

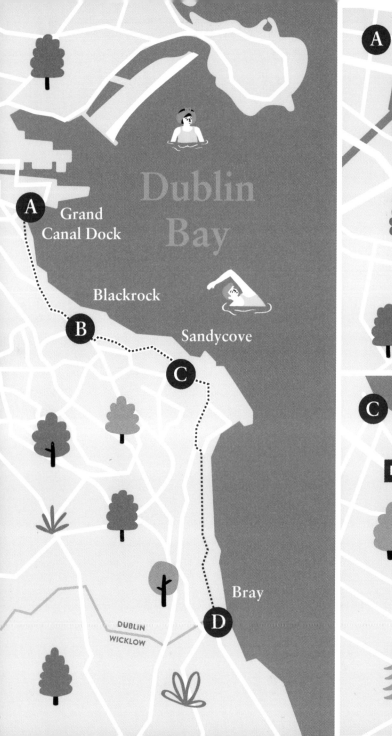

Dublin
Bay

Grand
Canal Dock

(A)

(B)

Blackrock

Sandycove

(C)

Bray

(D)

DUBLIN
WICKLOW

(A)

RINGSEND

DART

(C)

DART

ADELAIDE RD

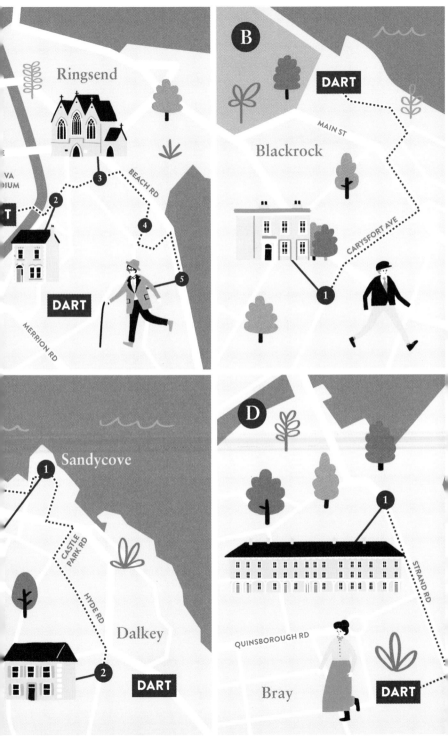

STOP A:
GRAND CANAL DOCK

① 60 Shelbourne Road

A short walk from Grand Canal Dock and you'll hit a set of modest terraced houses. Joyce rented number 60 for a few months in 1904, while back in Dublin following the death of his mother. The family home in Phibsborough was in disarray, as James's younger sister Poppie had taken over the running of the household, and John Joyce's drinking and abusive behaviour had only worsened. At the time Joyce was training for the Feis Ceoil, and his father had sold the family piano; he used this as an excuse to move closer to the city and procure one.

Joyce rented a large room at the top of the house, funded by loans from Oliver St. John

Gogarty, J. F. Byrne and George 'Æ' Russell, and immediately went about sourcing a piano. When the delivery men came he pretended not to be in, to avoid tipping them – but instead of leaving the piano, they took it back to the shop.

While living here, Joyce began writing and publishing the stories that would eventually become *Dubliners*. 'The Sisters', 'After the Race' and 'Eveline' all appeared in the *Irish Homestead* in 1904.

② 9 Newbridge Avenue

Passing the hulking Lansdowne Road stadium over the River Dodder, we reach the setting for the beginning of Paddy Dignam's funeral cortège in the 'Hades' episode of *Ulysses*. Described in the *Evening Telegraph* in the book, Dignam was 'a most popular and genial personality in city life and his demise, after a brief illness, came as a great shock to citizens of all classes by whom he is deeply regretted'.

It is said that Paddy Dignam was based on John Joyce's friend Matthew F. Kane, who died tragically on the 10th of June, 1904, from a stroke while swimming in Dún Laoghaire. His alcoholic wife had been committed to an asylum before his death, and he left five young children in his wake. Kane's own funeral cortège traipsed from Dún Laoghaire all the way to Glasnevin Cemetery, and many of the real-life attendees are name-checked at Dignam's fictional funeral too.

3 Star of the Sea Church, Sandymount

St. Mary's, Star of the Sea, Catholic Church, just off the main road in Sandymount, was built in 1851 and features several times in Joyce's writings. Most notably, it is a presence in the 'Nausicaa' episode of *Ulysses*, where Leopold Bloom surveys Cissy Caffrey and Edy Boardman as they struggle to keep their young brothers in check on Sandymount Strand, and lusts after the lame Gerty MacDowell with her 'rosebud mouth' and 'ivorylike purity'.

When the two ladies walk down to the strand to watch the fireworks from the opening of the nearby Mirus Bazaar, Gerty displays her legs for Bloom, who takes the opportunity to masturbate, his climax harmonising with the explosion of a Roman candle in the background:

And then a rocket sprang and bang shot blind blank and O! then the Roman candle burst and it was like a sigh of O! and everyone cried O! O! in raptures ...

⑤ Sandymount Strand

From the beach you can survey most of Dublin Bay, from the harbour at Dún Laoghaire all the way out to the peninsula of Howth. The strand features prominently in *Ulysses*, perhaps most famously in 'Proteus', where we're tossed inside the complex mind of Stephen Dedalus as he walks along the shore:

Stephen closed his eyes to hear his boots crush crackling wrack and shells. You are walking through it howsomever. I am, a stride at a time ... Am I walking into eternity along Sandymount strand? Crush, crack, crick, crick.

In the 'Hades' episode, Bloom spots Stephen 'clad in mourning, a wide hat' on the strand as he leaves in a cab for Paddy Dignam's funeral.

④ 22 Dromard Terrace

Having being kicked out of Shelbourne Road for failing to pay his rent, Joyce took up brief residence here, the home of his friends James and Gretta Cousins. James Cousins was a poet and playwright who moved in the circles of Æ and Yeats, and it is believed that he inspired the Little Chandler character from *Dubliners*. It was at this address that Joyce spent the night of the 16th of June, 1904, following his first walk with Nora.

During the summer of 1904 their relationship intensified, although, writing to her during this period, Joyce struggled to express his affection:

You ask me why I don't love you, but surely you must believe I am very fond of you and if to desire to possess a person wholly, to admire and honour that person deeply, and to seek to secure that person's happiness in every way is to 'love', then perhaps my affection for you is a kind of love.

To get to our next destination, we must visit another Joycean spot: Sydney Parade Railway Station. In 'A Painful Case' in *Dubliners*, this is the site of Mrs. Sinico's death when she is run down by a train while crossing the tracks. We suggest you stick to the platforms when heading to our next destination, Blackrock!

STOP B: BLACKROCK

1 23 Carysfort Avenue ('Leoville')

Just a short walk from the station leads you to this corner house, 'Leoville', the last southside address of the Joyce family. Following their move from here, the Joyces changed lodgings frequently, sometimes a few times in a year. But they managed to stick out almost the entirety of 1892 in this home.

The youngest surviving Joyce children, Florence and Mabel, were born here. James had been taken out of education at Clongowes Wood. He schooled himself, his mother examining him on lessons that he himself set!

Joyce portrays their removal from Leoville vividly in *A Portrait*...:

*Two great yellow caravans
had halted one morning before
the door and men had come
tramping into the house to
dismantle it. The furniture
had been hustled out through
the front garden which was
strewn with wisps of straw
and rope ends and into the
huge vans at the gate.*

STOP C:
SANDYCOVE/GLASTHULE

Hopping back on the DART,
you'll be able to access the
lovely villages of Sandycove and
Dalkey with ease. These spots
are the starting points for many
people celebrating Bloomsday,
and our first point of interest is
an address strongly associated
with Joyce and his work.

These quaint areas would
have been seen as respectable
in his time. In the *Dubliners*
story 'The Dead', Gabriel's
cousin Mary Jane gives music
lessons, and it is remarked that
'many of her pupils belonged to
the better-class families on the
Kingstown and Dalkey line'.

Sandycove also pops up
in grimmer circumstances in
the 'Lotus Eaters' episode of
Ulysses, when Bloom bumps
into his friend M'Coy. The
latter declares that he may not
be able to make it to Paddy
Dignam's funeral as 'there's a
drowning case at Sandycove may
turn up and then the coroner
and myself would have to go
down if a body is found'.

1 Martello Tower,
Sandycove

This tower was one of
sixteen built along the
Dublin coast in the early
1800s as a defence against a
Napoleonic invasion. (Only
nine remain standing today.)

Joyce lived in the fort for less
than a week in 1904 with his
acquaintances Oliver St. John
Gogarty and Samuel Chenevix

Trench, and his experiences here formed the basis for the opening episode of *Ulysses*, 'Telemachus'. Gogarty inspired the character of Buck Mulligan, while Trench became Haines. Joyce left on the 15th of September after Gogarty fired shots into the pots and pans hanging over Joyce's bed.

Today, the tower is home to the James Joyce Museum, where you can find some of his possessions such as his walking stick and guitar. His room has also been recreated. The museum was opened in 1962 by Joyce's friend and publisher Sylvia Beach.

2 The Clifton School, Summerfield Lodge

On the steep incline of Dalkey Avenue sits a large property with light-blue shutters. This impressive house was once a school, where Joyce held a position as a teacher from mid-May until the end of June 1904. It was during this period that he met Nora Barnacle.

Did You Know?

Joyce was plagued by two phobias: cynophobia (fear of dogs) and tonitrophobia (fear of thunder). It is said that the first was the result of his being bitten by a dog as a child (he was again attacked by a dog in Holland in 1927), and the second the result of the early religious influence of his governess Elizabeth Conway. Portrayed as 'Dante' in *A Portrait...*, Conway instilled in the young boy a fear of thunder by proclaiming it the angry voice of God.

The founder of the school, Denis Irwin, appears in *Ulysses* as Mr. Deasy, whose school provides the backdrop for the 'Nestor' episode.

He went out by the open porch and down the gravel path under the trees, hearing the cries of voices and crack of sticks from the playfield. The lions couchant on the pillars as he passed out through the gate; toothless terrors.

Today, the house belongs to Barry Devlin, who was the lead singer of Irish band Horslips.

STOP D: BRAY

As a bonus to finish off this trail, you can hop back on the DART and head to Bray in neighbouring County Wicklow. The Joyces moved to this lovely seaside town in 1887 and remained for almost four years. It features most notably in *A Portrait…* as the setting for the Christmas-dinner scene in which talk of Parnell results in an explosive argument.

1 1 Martello Terrace

Number 1 was the Joyces' first coastal address. It was located just far enough from Dublin city that John Joyce felt it would deter frequent visits from his wife's relatives, about whom he complained that 'the name of Murray stank in his nostrils'! That said, he encouraged friends to come and stay whenever they liked. He even hosted lodgers who were fresh out of prison to recuperate from their incarceration.

The house was full of music, with James's mother May singing and playing the piano and his brother Stanislaus singing 'Finnegan's Wake' as his tune of choice. During their time here, four more Joyce siblings were born: George, Eileen, Mary and Eva. When James turned six, he was packed off from Martello Terrace to attend boarding school at Clongowes Wood in Kildare.

The North Coastal Suburbs

*Welcome, O life, I go to encounter for the millionth
time the reality of experience and to forge in the smithy
of my soul the uncreated conscience of my race.*

Joyce's family lived in various parts of the north coastal
suburbs during his university years. Anecdotes, addresses and
other details from the time he spent in the area are found in
abundance in *A Portrait of the Artist as a Young Man,* as Joyce's
alter ego Stephen Dedalus's movements mirror those of the
author himself. Joyce liked to take 'preposterously long walks'
from his home near the North Strand Road through Fairview
and along Dollymount Strand. Following in his footsteps, we'll
hit up all the abodes that the Joyces traipsed between from
1898–1901, building up a picture of what this part of Dublin
was like at the turn of the 20th Century.

The first part of this trail can be done on foot; after that, we
recommend you hop on a bike or a DART to travel to the
picturesque fishing village of Howth.

DART

DART

8 DART

Howth

Dollymount
Strand

Dublin Bay

1 North Strand Road

This road leads you directly into Fairview and a hive of Joycean homes from the turn of the 19th Century. It is also the main link between the north inner city and the northern suburbs. It features most prominently in 'An Encounter' in *Dubliners*:

We walked along the North Strand Road till we came to the Vitriol Works and then turned to the right along the Wharf Road. Mahony began to play the Indian as soon as we were out of public sight. He chased a crowd of ragged girls, brandishing his unloaded catapult and, when two ragged boys began, out of chivalry, to fling stones at us, he proposed that we should charge them.

The Vitriol Works was a landmark plant in Dublin at that time, 'vitriol' being another name for sulphuric acid, which was used in the leather industry. The ragged boys and girls would have been poor children who were likely fed, clothed and educated by Catholic charities in the area.

2 Fairview

At the end of North Strand Road, you'll enter Fairview itself. This suburb began to develop in 1797, when the Annesley Bridge was built over the River Tolka. These days, Fairview is punctuated by a large park, but when Joyce and his family were residents, it was effectively a landfill known as the sloblands:

His morning walk across the city had begun, and he foreknew that as he passed the sloblands of Fairview …

The Joyces moved to four different houses around this area between 1898 and 1901, sometimes inhabiting their own home and sometimes sharing with other families. John Joyce had retired and was spending much of his pension and his inheritance on drink. These were also the last few years that Joyce's mother was alive.

③ 29 Windsor Avenue

This narrow street beside the park was home to the Joyces from 1898 until 1899. While living here, May Joyce had a stillborn son who remained unnamed. James Joyce would have been in his first year of university and made the three-mile pilgrimage into town by foot every day to pursue his studies.

During this time, the Joyces were repeatedly evicted for not paying their rent. John Joyce was disdainful of the concept of rent, and according to James's brother Stanislaus, their father believed that it was just to charge for food but unjust to demand 'exorbitant sums' for shelter. As a result, he devised cunning plans to avoid paying rent but still obtain a new lease once they had been evicted. As you'll note, these houses were all so near to one another it's surprising that landlords didn't catch on to Joyce's schemes.

④ 8 Royal Terrace (now Inverness Road)

Just a two-minute walk from Windsor Avenue, this is where the Joyces filled in the 1901 census on the night of March 31st. At that time there were ten children living in the house; John Joyce was aged 51, and May Joyce was 41. Two years later she died of liver cancer.

It was here that James Joyce sent off his play *A Brilliant*

Career (now lost) to William Archer, Henrik Ibsen's first English translator, for approval. It was the only work he ever dedicated to anyone, and he dedicated it to himself:

—To—
*My own Soul I
dedicate the first
true work of my
life*

The garden of this house is overlooked by the nearby St. Vincent's psychiatric hospital. In *A Portrait...*, Stephen enters the lane behind the garden and hears 'a mad nun screeching in the nuns' madhouse beyond the wall'.

⑤ Convent Avenue

Just as Joyce was finishing his first year at university, the family made another abrupt move around the corner to Convent Avenue. This time they shared their home with a family named Hughes, with the three Hugheses making

way for the twelve Joyces.

By this point, John Joyce's rent-avoidance scams were in full swing. One method he used was to ask each landlord who evicted them to provide a fake receipt for the rent, so the Joyces could move out quickly and avoid expensive legal proceedings. John Joyce would then present this receipt to the next unsuspecting landlord and wheedle his way into another non–rent paying situation.

During these frequent moves, the family portraits would be carried by hand, as they were considered their most valuable assets. All their other belongings, which dwindled in size each time they moved, were put on floats.

⑥ 13 Richmond Avenue

The family's next home almost backs onto the one on Inverness Road. The Joyces shared this house with a family from Ulster for less than a year. During this time, Joyce's interest in

Henrik Ibsen afforded him a prestigious opportunity: Ibsen's latest play, *When We Dead Awaken*, had just been published, and in early 1900, Joyce submitted an article on it to *The Fortnightly Review*, one of the most influential magazines in England at the time.

Joyce received praise from William Archer for the article, as well as the princely sum of twelve guineas. He used his earnings to take his father on a trip to London, where they went to theatres and dance halls and met with Archer in person to discuss Joyce's budding literary career.

7 Dollymount Strand

A short walk from Joyce's Fairview homes, you'll come to one of the longest stretches of sandy beach in the capital.

It features in an important scene in *A Portrait*...:

He turned seaward from the road at Dollymount and as he passed on to the thin wooden bridge he felt the planks shaking with the tramp of heavily shod feet. A squad of Christian Brothers was on its way back from the Bull and had begun to pass, two by two, across the bridge. Soon the whole bridge was trembling and resounding.

Stephen had just considered the possibility that he might become a priest, so this moment is salient for him. It is also here that he catches sight of a beautiful girl, 'her thighs, fuller and soft-hued as ivory, were bared almost to the hips, where the white fringes of her drawers were like featherings of soft white down'. Entranced, Stephen walks further out onto the strand, considering the 'angel of mortal youth and beauty' that he has just encountered, further rejecting the life of chastity and piety that had been set out for him.

59

8 Howth

On the other side of lovely St. Anne's Park is Raheny DART station, where you can start the short train journey to Howth. Back in Joyce's day, Howth was a seaside resort for well-to-do city dwellers, something that he makes reference to in 'A Mother' in *Dubliners*:

Every year in the month of July Mrs. Kearney found occasion to say to some friend: 'My good man is packing us off to Skerries for a few weeks.' If it was not Skerries it was Howth or Greystones.

Howth Head is famously referred to in the final episode of *Ulysses*, 'Penelope', when Molly recounts reclining on the hill with Leopold just before he proposes to her:

... we were lying among the rhododendrons on Howth head in the grey tweed suit and his straw hat the day I got him to propose to me yes first I gave him the bit of seedcake out of my mouth and it was leapyear like now yes 16 years ago my God after that long kiss I near lost my breath ...

It is possible to walk up to the top of Howth Head from the village (or hop on the 31/a bus) to take in the stunning views that attracted the young Blooms. As you cast your eye from the Baily Lighthouse across the bay to Ireland's Eye, keep in mind that in *Finnegans Wake*, Howth also represents the head of sleeping giant Finn MacCool, whose body makes up the North Dublin landscape: 'he was obliffious of the headth of hosth that rosed before him.'

The North City Suburbs

*He heard the choir of voices in the kitchen echoed and
multiplied through an endless reverberation of the choirs of
endless generations of children and heard in all the echoes
an echo also of the recurring note of weariness and pain.
All seemed weary of life even before entering upon it.*

This trail around Phibsborough, Glasnevin and Drumcondra
represents a dark time in both Joyce's life and in the parallel
universe of *Ulysses*. He spent parts of his youth living in the
area, and as in the 'Hades' episode of the book, death was a
dominant theme that followed the Joyces through this part of
Dublin. John Joyce's alcoholism had taken a darker turn, and he
would repeatedly lash out at members of the family.

We begin at the last address that James would share with his
father, a home purchased by John Joyce in 1902. This was
also the place where James Joyce spent the last few months
of his time in Dublin before deciding to exile himself from
Ireland for good.

RIVER TOLKA

AVE

MILLBOURNE AVE

5

IONA RD

4

DRUMCONDRA RD

DRUMCONDRA

Drumcondra

ROYAL CANAL

DORSET ST

NORTH CIRCULAR RD

1 7 St. Peter's Terrace (now 5 St. Peter's Road)

The Joyces purchased this house in October 1902. John Joyce decided that his children were reaching an age where they no longer required support, so he cashed in his pension to buy the property. However, this proved to be a pretty dire move, with six daughters and three sons to provide for on a monthly sum of £5 and 10 shillings. The family was quickly plunged back into poverty; Stanislaus referred to this as the 'house of the bare table'.

It was also here that Joyce's mother, May, died of liver cancer on the 13th of August, 1903. Joyce was living in Paris at the time but returned to Dublin when he received an urgent, misspelled telegram: 'Nother dying come home father.'

While back home, he began work on the first iteration of *A Portrait of the Artist as a Young Man*, then a 63-chapter autobiographical novel called *Stephen Hero*.

2 Dunphy's Corner (Doyle's Corner)

Heading back towards Drumcondra along the North Circular Road, we hit what is now called Doyle's Corner. Leopold Bloom passes what was then Dunphy's Corner while in Paddy Dignam's funeral cortège in the 'Hades' episode of *Ulysses*. He remarks that it's a 'tiptop position for a pub' and postulates that the group will probably stop there afterwards to drink to Dignam's memory. His mind then drifts to a darker place, wondering if Dignam's body would still bleed if cut. Bloom decides it would be better if bodies were buried in dark-red material.

This intersection is one of several in Dublin named after the pubs that were located there. John Doyle's – which you can see on the right-hand side of the intersection as you face Glasnevin – would have been Dunphy's pub in Joyce's time.

3 32 (now 10) Glengarriff Parade

Moving further along the North Circular Road and taking a left, we reach another rather sombre former residence. This house was originally number 32 when the Joyces moved in in late 1901. These attractive bay-windowed cottages are overlooked by the grim Mountjoy Prison.

In early 1902, Joyce's

younger brother George became ill with typhoid while living here. Their mother agonised over whether to bring him to hospital or nurse him at home. When a doctor finally came, he declared George to be out of the woods and advised May that she could feed him whatever she wanted. Unfortunately, this diagnosis would prove fatal, and George died shortly afterwards from an inflammation of the abdomen. The death affected the family deeply, and Joyce modelled the tragic character of Isabel in *Stephen Hero* on his younger brother.

4 Drumcondra Road

Continuing up into Drumcondra, we pass what would have been a terminus for the city's expansive tram system in the late 1800s – a system that coils and winds its way across Joyce's

65

Dublin. For instance, in the *Dubliners* story 'Clay', Maria takes the tram from Ballsbridge to Drumcondra to see Joe, a now grown-up boy that she once nannied. She alights just before the canal bridge with a bag of cakes she purchased to make a good impression. As she makes her way to the nearby house, she realises she has misplaced the most important cake, which causes her great distress. During the evening she tries to talk to Joe about his strained relations with his brother Alphy.

Joe cried that God might strike him stone dead if ever he spoke a word to his brother again.

The characters of Joe and Alphy were supposedly based on Joyce's uncles William and John Murray.

5 **2 Millbourne Avenue**

Just off Drumcondra Road Lower, we hit the site of another Joyce family home, sadly now demolished. The Joyces moved to number 2 in March 1894; it was characterised by James's brother Stanislaus as a 'bleak house'. It certainly lived up to this reputation: a new Joyce, Freddie, was born here in the summer but survived for only a few weeks. Shortly afterwards John Joyce attempted to strangle May, grabbing her throat in a fit of drunken rage. According to Stanislaus, it was James who saved her by jumping on his father's back and toppling them both over.

As if things weren't bad enough, it was also while living at this address that Joyce was

6 Hedigan's/The Brian Boru

We take a brief detour now, heading back towards the city centre via the Brian Boru Pub on Prospect Road. This building has rich historical ties with Dublin and features in the 'Hades' episode of *Ulysses*, as the mourners at Paddy Dignam's funeral make their way to Glasnevin Cemetery.

They drove on past the Brian Boroimhe House. Near it now.

It was first founded in the 1840s as a public house and greengrocers, and is said to be built on the spot where Brian Boru – the High King of Ireland in the 11th Century – camped with his army before the Battle of Clontarf in 1014. With a recurring cast of fallen leaders and references to chaotic battles, it is no surprise to find allusions to Clontarf ('Bull on clompturf', Clontarf meaning 'Bull's Meadow') and Boru himself ('Urp, Boohooru!') woven into the tapestry of *Finnegans Wake*.

beaten up in nearby Griffith Park by his classmates. The episode, recounted in *A Portrait...*, arose from an argument over who was the better poet, Tennyson or Byron. Stephen stumps for Byron and pays the price for his convictions!

7 Glasnevin Cemetery

The last stop on this trail is the final resting place of Joyce's mother, father and siblings. Glasnevin Cemetery was established in 1832 and is Ireland's largest, with over 1.5 million people buried here, including famous national figures such as Charles Stewart Parnell and Daniel O'Connell. It is also the setting for Paddy Dignam's funeral during the 'Hades' episode of *Ulysses*.

While Bloom awaits the burial of the body, he begins to have all manner of unsavoury thoughts about the bodies lying in the earth beneath him:

I daresay the soil would be quite fat with corpse manure, bones, flesh, nails, charnelhouses. Dreadful. Turning green and pink, decomposing ...

Joyce attended plenty of family members' funerals here at Glasnevin, except that of his father, who died on the 29th of December, 1931. He sent a wreath in his stead. Despite this seemingly uncaring gesture, he wrote to T.S. Eliot and Ezra Pound at the time expressing his regret and remorse at his father's death, explaining, 'I feel that a poor heart which was true and faithful to me is no more.'

The Phoenix Park & Environs

Mr. James Duffy lived in Chapelizod … He lived in an old sombre house and from his windows he could look into the disused distillery or upwards along the shallow river on which Dublin was built.

This trail begins in the sleepy village of Chapelizod, which lies beside the River Liffey and the great expanse of Phoenix Park. The name comes from the 'Chapel of Isolde' from Arthurian times. Chapelizod was the setting for Joseph Sheridan Le Fanu's *The House by the Churchyard*, published in 1863 and alluded to by Joyce in *Finnegans Wake*. In the book, Joyce refers to the village as everything from 'Cheepalizzy's' and 'Izd-la-Chapelle' to 'Shop Illicit' and a 'couple of lizards'.

In the *Dubliners* story 'A Painful Case', protagonist Mr. Duffy chooses Chapelizod as his home 'because he wished to live as far as possible from the city of which he was a citizen and because he found all other suburbs of Dublin mean, modern and pretentious'. The River Liffey also features as a main character in *Finnegans Wake*, under the name Anna Livia Plurabelle, amongst others.

ROYAL CANAL

Cabra

NAVAN RD

ÁRAS AN
UACHTARÁIN

DUBLIN
ZOO

7

CHAPELIZOD RD

RIVER LIFFEY

HEUSTON STATION

IRISH MUSEUM
OF MODERN ART

Kilmainham

1 The House by the Churchyard, 34 Martin's Row

This trail begins at a spot that had a heavy influence on another writer and, subsequently, on Joyce himself.

The House by the Churchyard is not only a novel by Joseph Sheridan Le Fanu but also a real building on windy Martin's Row, which snakes around the periphery of the Phoenix Park and borders the Liffey. This tall and thin grey building with its stark black door frame and white door gives off exactly the kind of spooky feeling that Le Fanu tries to evoke in his murder mystery about the lives, loves and disagreements of the residents of Chapelizod.

In *Finnegans Wake* Joyce utilises a lot of the same character names as Le Fanu and incorporates their ghosts into the text.

2 Old Distillery (Phoenix Park Distillery)

Turning away from this house and crossing the road, we find ourselves on a prim, flagstoned triangle that would have been home to a thriving distillery in Joyce's day. In *Finnegans Wake* Joyce refers to it as 'the still that was the mill', due to its previous incarnation as a linen mill. The white house that sits just down the steps from the paved plaza still bears the plaque 'Distillery House'.

John Joyce was involved with the distillery here before James was born. Having negotiated a buy-in with a Cork man, Henry Alleyn, in exchange for a job as the company secretary, John lived and worked in Chapelizod in the late 1870s. He later became the trustee of the distillery, having outed Alleyn as cheating the business. Unfortunately, at that point, he was trustee of nothing as all the money was gone. James Joyce later included a mean managerial character named Mr. Alleyne in his *Dubliners* story 'Counterparts', no doubt as a hat tip to his father's erstwhile employer.

It was also at the distillery that John Joyce first encountered John Murray, the father of his wife-to-be, May, when he came to purchase spirits there.

③ The Bridge Inn, St. Laurence's Road

Take tiny Maiden's Row and St. Laurence's Road down to the Bridge Inn, a handsome red-brick corner building that looks like it's part of the bridge itself.

This is the venue in which Mr. Duffy takes a drink to steady his nerves after hearing about the death of a former acquaintance, Mrs. Sinico, in 'A Painful Case':

The shock which had first attacked his stomach was now attacking his nerves. He put on his overcoat and hat quickly and went out … When he came to the public-house at Chapelizod Bridge he went in and ordered a hot punch.

As we'll see at our next stop, it is commonly believed that Mullingar House is the spot of HCE's tavern in *Finnegans Wake*, but there are also references to it as the 'Bristol'. In old English, a bristol was a bridge, and so there's another theory that the Bridge Inn plays the role of the Earwicker pub.

4 Mullingar House, Chapelizod Road

At the opposite end of St. Laurence's Road, where it meets Chapelizod Road, we see Mullingar House. In John Joyce's day, it was the Mullingar Hotel, and during his time working for the distillery he became acquainted with its owner, Broadbent.

Anecdotes about Broadbent would serve as inspiration for Humphrey Chimpden Earwicker (or HCE), the main character in Joyce's final work. The pub that HCE manages in the book takes on various locations and forms, but one of these is said to be this unassuming bar.

Today, Mullingar House bears a plaque making the ballsy claim that it is 'home of all characters and elements in James Joyce's novel *Finnegans*

Wake', and you can enjoy your lunch in their very own James Joyce Bistro.

6 The Hole in the Wall Pub

Making your way directly across the huge, green expanse of Phoenix Park, you'll arrive at the Blackhorse Avenue exit and a well-preserved coach house that began its life in the 1600s. Originally called the Blackhorse Tavern, it gained the nickname of the Hole in the Wall in the late 1800s, as that was the method used to serve drinks to British soldiers who were forbidden from leaving the park. It is also referred to as 'Nancy Hands' in *Finnegans Wake*, after the woman who acted as its proprietor around this time.

In the book, Nancy Hands is sometimes combined with the character of Anna

5 Phoenix Park

Doubling back northwest, we soon come to the Chapelizod Gate of Phoenix Park. This gigantic urban park houses the president of Ireland, a grand mansion called Farmleigh and a zoo, and counts herds of wild deer amongst its residents.

Finnegans Wake alludes to the park regularly, often relating it to the Garden of Eden. Joyce references the clearly visible obelisk of the Wellington Monument, the lions in Dublin Zoo, and even the 'fionn-uisge spring' that gave Phoenix Park its name (thanks to a mistranslation). The park itself is mutated into 'Fiendish park', 'Finnish pork', 'Finest Park' and 'fenian's bark'.

Gabriel Conroy also thinks about the Wellington Monument in 'The Dead', dreaming of escaping the hot and stuffy surrounds of the Morkans' party:

How pleasant it would be to walk out alone, first along by the river and then through the park! The snow would be lying on the branches of the trees and forming a bright cap on the top of the Wellington Monument.

Livia Plurabelle, who is simultaneously the wife of HCE and the River Liffey.

Beginning your trek back towards the city centre, the final stop on this trail is right beside the banks of the Liffey, which has now widened out from its humble beginnings in Chapelizod.

7 Collins Barracks, the National Museum of Ireland

One of the oldest public buildings in Dublin, dating back to 1701, this is now home to the Decorative Arts & History wing of the National Museum of Ireland. In Joyce's time the barracks were falling into disrepair for the remaining British troops stationed there, and disease was rife.

Today, the museum houses the reclining buddha, a remnant of the Imperial era (it was looted from Burma) and one which is alluded to in *Ulysses*. In the 'Lotus Eaters' episode, Bloom recalls seeing it at its former home of the National Museum on Kildare Street: 'Buddha their God lying on his side in the museum. Taking it easy with hand under his cheek.' Molly Bloom later recalls Leopold bringing her to see the statue 'all yellow in a pinafore, lying on his side on his hand with his ten toes sticking out'.

Where to next?

For readers of Joyce, and particularly those taking their first plunge, the shelves of books about the author can appear pretty daunting. But there are so many things to discover – so many ways into the work – that the numerous books and films, apps and websites dedicated to Joyce should be seen as a support network for readers. Here's a small selection of some of the best companions on your Joycean journey.

The standard biography, *James Joyce* by Richard Ellmann, remains unsurpassed. Although almost one thousand pages, it's a rollicking read and an astonishing portrait of this one-of-a-kind artist. If you don't want to weigh down your backpack, there are some excellent shorter biographies, such as *James Joyce: A Life* by Edna O'Brien and *James Joyce (Very Interesting People)* by Bruce Stewart.

Joyce's remark that he would 'keep the professors busy for centuries' seems (so far at least) to be spot on, as you consider the many guides to his work that are out there. Excellent scholarly companions such as Don Gifford's *Ulysses Annotated* and Terence Killeen's *Ulysses Unbound*, or Roland McHugh's *Annotations to Finnegans Wake* and John Bishop's *Joyce's Book of the Dark*, are complemented by lighter guides such as the *Digital Dubliners* app, Rob Berry's graphic novel adaptation *Ulysses "Seen"* and the *Romping Through ...* series by At it Again!

We must also recommend Robert Nicholson's *The Ulysses Guide* and *James Joyce's Dublin Houses* by Vivien Igoe. The graphic guide *Introducing Joyce* by Senator David Norris, a resident of North Great George's Street and founder of the James Joyce Centre, is both witty and intellectually stimulating.

And of course, don't forget Joyce himself. Sometimes there's nothing better than to take a bath in the musical 'jingle jaunty jingle' of his work and see where it takes you.

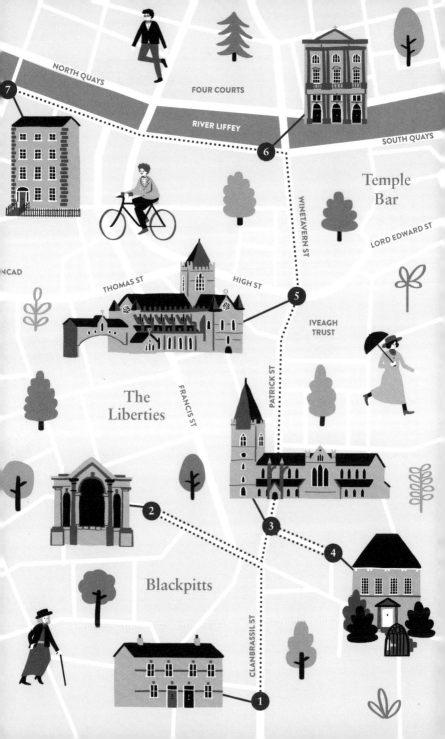

NORTH QUAYS

FOUR COURTS

RIVER LIFFEY

SOUTH QUAYS

7

6

Temple
Bar

LORD EDWARD ST

WINETAVERN ST

NCAD

THOMAS ST

HIGH ST

5

IVEAGH
TRUST

PATRICK ST

The
Liberties

FRANCIS ST

2

3

4

Blackpitts

CLANBRASSIL ST

1

The Viking Heart

The rain had drawn off; and amid the moving vapours
from point to point of light the city was spinning
about herself a soft cocoon of yellowish haze.

This trail is based around Dublin's Viking heart, the oldest part
of the city, which is peppered with Joycean associations and
home to 15 Usher's Island, the backdrop for his most famous
short story, 'The Dead'.

Several of these places are referenced only obliquely in his
work; here we will attempt to unpack some of these allusions
and provide some background to their real-life locations. These
include Dublin's main cathedrals, as well as one of the capital's
hidden gems, Marsh's Library. But first we will begin at the
former home of James Joyce's mother, May Murray.

① 7 Clanbrassil St. Lower

At the opposite end of Clanbrassil Street to the house associated with the birth of Leopold Bloom, you'll find the site of the family home of the Murrays. Sadly this building no longer exists, but you can get a sense of what it would have looked like from nearby numbers 11 and 12.

This is where May was living when she met John Joyce, and he quickly set about wooing her. The Murrays weren't as passionate about their future son-in-law – there was even an altercation on Grafton Street when May's father caught them out together! John Joyce, undeterred, made his intentions clear by moving into number 15 Clanbrassil Street so as to be closer to his love. His future

mother-in-law encouraged the pair to marry. When they finally did so, in 1880, only John Joyce's mother still opposed the union, as she considered the Murrays to be 'beneath her'.

② The Coombe

Turning left at the crossroads before St. Patrick's Cathedral, we enter an area that is cited several times, often unflatteringly, in *Ulysses*. In 'Lotus Eaters' Bloom refers to 'two sluts that night in the Coombe' and in the 'Circe' chapter, set in Dublin's red-light district, the same two women pop up again:

Two sluts of the Coombe dance rainily by, shawled, yelling flatly.

During the 'Lestrygonians' episode, Bloom spots an acquaintance, Bob Doran,

3 St. Patrick's Cathedral

During one of Bloom's feverish hallucinations in the 'Circe' episode of *Ulysses*, he imagines the bells of this grand cathedral ringing out during his coronation:

Bloom assumes a mantle of cloth of gold and puts on a ruby ring. He ascends and stands on the stone of destiny. The representative peers put on at the same time their twentyeight crowns. Joybells ring in Christ church, Saint Patrick's, George's and gay Malahide.

An Anglican cathedral since the 16th Century, St. Patrick's would have been one of the city's best-known landmarks in Joyce's day. According to Andrew Smith, the cathedral's Education Officer, in the early 20th Century it was a hub of cultural activity. Queen Victoria visited during her stay in Dublin in 1900, and it had many literary associations. The Dean, John Henry Bernard, continued the tradition of previous deans such as Jonathan Swift by writing extensively. Future precentor of the cathedral Arthur Aston Luce published work on Irish philosopher George Berkeley. And W.B. Yeats, inspired by St. Patrick's, wrote a one-act play called *Words Upon the Window Pane*, in which he imagines communicating with Jonathan Swift.

who appears throughout the book on his 'annual bender'. He recalls an earlier remark that Doran hits the bottle ...

... in order to say or do something or cherchez la femme. Up in the Coombe with chummies and streetwalkers and then the rest of the year sober as a judge.

Nearby Marrowbone Lane also pops into Molly's head during her long and winding soliloquy, as she remembers dirty jokes being told to her by 'cornerboys' on the lane:

... my uncle John has a thing long I heard those cornerboys saying passing the corner of Marrowbone lane my aunt Mary has a thing hairy ...

④ Marsh's Library

Situated within the grounds of St. Patrick's Cathedral is Marsh's Library. Joyce spent some time in 1902 researching books in these hallowed halls. The library obviously had an effect on him, as it is referred to in a number of his works. In *Ulysses*, Stephen recalls 'the stagnant bay of Marsh's library' where he read 'the fading prophecies of Joachim Abbas'.

Joyce would also recall his time here in *Stephen Hero*, where Stephen 'came on an old library in the midst of those sluttish streets which are called old Dublin'. He also remarks on how 'few people seemed aware of its existence'.

According to Dr. Jason McElligott, the Keeper of Marsh's Library, Joyce was drawn here in part to access books by radical monks like Joachim Abbas, which were not available in institutions like the National Library or Newman House. Today visitors to Marsh's Library can sit in the very chairs, and at the very table, which Joyce used in 1902.

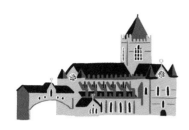

Joyce uses them as a simile in *Finnegans Wake*, describing one character as 'as stuck as that cat to that mouse in that tube of that christchurch organ'.

5 Christ Church

A short walk uphill towards the Liffey brings you to one of the city's most recognisable landmarks. Christ Church Cathedral is Dublin's oldest and certainly one of its most stunning churches, set in the heart of the medieval quarter on Wood Quay. Founded in 1030 by the fabulously named King Sitric Silkenbeard, it has a crypt underneath that is the largest of its kind in Britain and Ireland.

It is in this crypt that the famous mummified bodies of the cat and the rat (or 'Tom and Jerry', as they are affectionately called) can be found. Discovered in an organ pipe in the 1850s, this perfectly preserved pair became stuck while in the midst of a chase and are now kept in a glass viewing case.

6 Adam & Eve's Church

As you walk down Winetavern Street and onto the quays, you'll quickly happen upon the Church of the Immaculate Conception, or Adam and Eve's, on Merchant's Quay. This Catholic church, run by the Franciscans, is the first place mentioned in the opening line of *Finnegans Wake* (often the only line people ever make it through!), which describes the flow of the River Liffey through the city:

riverrun, past Eve and Adam's, from swerve of shore to bend of bay, brings us by a commodius vicus of recirculation back to Howth Castle and Environs.

The grey-stone front blends in with the façades of the other buildings on the quays, and only its wooden doors and short steps make the distinction that this is a church building. Joyce also makes reference to it in 'The Dead', saying of Aunt Julia: 'though she was quite grey, [she] was still the leading soprano in Adam and Eve's'.

7 15 Usher's Island

This trail ends at an address that has strong associations with Joyce and his work. Number 15 Usher's Island serves as the setting of perhaps his best-known short story, 'The Dead'. In the tale the Misses Morkan host an evening of dinner, dancing and drinks in celebration of the Feast of the Epiphany.

For years and years it had gone off in splendid style as long as anyone could remember; ever since Kate and Julia, after the death of their brother Pat, had left the house in Stoney Batter and taken Mary Jane, their only niece, to live with them in the dark gaunt house on Usher's Island.

In this story, the last and longest of *Dubliners*, Joyce depicted the city's 'ingenuous insularity and … hospitality'. In this respect, 'The Dead' stands in contrast with the other stories in the collection, as Joyce privately wondered to Stanislaus if he had not been 'unnecessarily harsh' in his depiction of Ireland.

In real life, this is where Joyce's mother, May Murray, received music and singing lessons as a child from her aunts at the Misses Flynn School. Although the house is now privately owned, it is possible on occasion to visit.

Joycean Pub Crawl

*Good puzzle would be cross
Dublin without passing a pub.*

On our final trail, we'll unwind a little bit with an exploration
of Dublin's public houses – the focal points for many scenes in
Joyce's work. The author knew the geography of Dublin's pubs
well, so it is of little surprise that so many significant episodes
across his work take place in pubs.

Many of the places that Joyce himself drank in, or that he
references in his works, are still in service today. This tour will
take you to some of the city's oldest watering holes and past
other establishments that have unfortunately disappeared with
the sands of time.

All of these bars are situated in the city centre, within walking
distance of one another, and since several have closed, you
could conceivably have a drink in each of the remaining pubs
over an evening.

Smithfield

CAPEL ST

No
In
C

9

FOUR COURTS

8

RIVER LIFFEY

7

CHRISTCHURCH

THE NORSEMAN

DUBLIN
CASTLE

HIGH ST

1

2

GPO

O'CONNELL ST

CUSTOMS HOUSE

3

DART

4

SOUTH QUAYS

Temple Bar

DAME ST

JOHN MULLIGAN LOUNGE BAR MULLIGANS

Trinity College

21

DAVY BYRNES

5

NASSAU ST

① The Gresham Hotel, O'Connell St.

Not strictly a pub but a good spot to grab a
drink, the Gresham Hotel is the setting for the
final climatic scene of Joyce's 'The Dead'.
After spending the evening at the Misses Morkan's annual
dinner on Usher's Island, Gabriel and Gretta Conroy retire
for the night to the Gresham, where Gretta tells her husband
the story of a romance from her youth in Galway. Gretta's
description of the now-dead Michael Furey, the young boy
who travelled to see her on a wet and freezing night while
he was gravely ill, inspires jealousy and anger in Gabriel,
who feels he can never live up to this ghost from her past.
As he watches the snow fall on O'Connell Street through
the window, Gabriel experiences the revelatory epiphany
that closes Joyce's collection of fifteen stories written
in his distinct style of 'scrupulous meanness':

*Generous tears filled Gabriel's eyes. He had never felt like that
himself towards any woman but he knew that such a feeling
must be love … His soul swooned slowly as he heard the snow
falling faintly through the universe and faintly falling, like the
descent of their last end, upon all the living and the dead.*

② The Oval, Middle Abbey St.

As you head down O'Connell Street towards the Liffey, you'll find the Oval Bar on the corner of Middle Abbey Street. Established in 1822, this bar has retained a wonderful character and heritage.

This spot marks the end of the 'Aeolus' episode of *Ulysses*, with the primary action taking place in the offices of the *Evening Telegraph* and *The Freeman's Journal*. Bloom heads there to discuss placing an ad, and while in pestering the editor, two of his acquaintances, Simon Dedalus and Ned Lambert, decide to hit the Oval, despite the early hour of the day:

③ The Scotch House, 6–8 Burgh Quay

Rain was drizzling down on the cold streets and, when they reached the Ballast Office, Farrington suggested the Scotch House. The bar was full of men and loud with the noise of tongues and glasses. The three men pushed past the whining match-sellers at the door and formed a little party at the corner of the counter.

The Scotch House once towered over the Liffey on Burgh Quay. Interestingly Davy Byrne – whose pub we'll visit later in this trail – cut his teeth as a bar manager here in the 1880s before heading further south of the

Liffey to open his own premises.

In the *Dubliners* story 'Counterparts', quoted here, this is one of the pubs that Farrington frequents on his self-loathing pub crawl. It was also popular with poets, journalists and artists during Joyce's time and later became known as the 'office' of Brian O'Nolan (better known by his penname, Flann O'Brien).

❹ Mulligan's, 8 Poolbeg St.

This pub has been operating for nearly three hundred years, making it one of the city's oldest. It was rumoured to be among Joyce's favourite haunts, and the owners have now taken the liberty of claiming he even spent time writing here!

It provides the backdrop for part of the 'Counterparts' story

in *Dubliners*, where the churlish Farrington sets out to drink, having pawned his watch for booze money. He spends much of the story concerned with how much he can spend on drinks and whether or not he's being defrauded by his companions:

He watched her leave the room in the hope that she would look back at him, but he was disappointed. He cursed his want of money and cursed all the rounds he had stood, particularly all the whiskies and Apollinaris which he had stood to Weathers. If there was one thing that he hated it was a sponge.

❻ The Norseman, 28 Eustace St.

Sitting right in the heart of Temple Bar, this pub was until

⑤ Davy Byrne's, 21 Duke St.

This bar just off Grafton Street features in many
of Joyce's works, as does its proprietor of the
day and namesake, Davy Byrne himself.
In October 1904, when Joyce was due to elope to Zurich with
Nora Barnacle, he made one last pilgrimage here to meet his
friend James Starkey, who was bringing him some necessary
toiletries from his father's pharmacy before he departed.
In *Ulysses*, the 'Lestrygonians' episode sees Bloom
adjourn to this 'moral pub' for a gorgonzola
sandwich and glass of burgundy at the bar:

*Mr. Bloom ate his strips of sandwich, fresh clean bread,
with relish of disgust, pungent mustard, the feety savour
of green cheese. Sips of his wine soothed his palate. Not
logwood that. Tastes fuller this weather with the chill off.
Nice quiet bar. Nice piece of wood in that counter.
Nicely planned. Like the way it curves there.*

recently named Farrington's
after the Joycean character. In
'Counterparts', it is referred to
as O'Neills and is the first pub
Farrington ducks into on his
lunchbreak at the beginning of
the story. He spends the rest
of his day figuring out how to
drink as much as possible for
as little as possible. He begins
with a 'g.p.' in O'Neill's:

*The curate brought him a glass
of plain porter. The man drank
it at a gulp and asked for a
caraway seed. He put his penny
on the counter and, leaving
the curate to grope for it in the
gloom, retreated out of the snug
as furtively as he had entered it.*

Farrington heads back to work
for an afternoon of anxiety and
belittlement, interrupted by 'his
great body again aching for the
comfort of the public-house'.

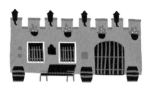

⑦ The Brazen Head, Bridge St. Lower

Located in the heart of old
Viking Dublin, on the corner
of Usher's Quay, this claims to
be Ireland's oldest pub. With a
founding date of 1198, it makes
Mulligan's seem a mere pup in
comparison. It is endorsed by
the character of Corley in the
'Eumaeus' episode of *Ulysses*,
although he gets the address
wrong – presumably because
he's had one too many!

*There was a dosshouse in
Marlborough street, Mrs.
Maloney's, but it was only
a tanner touch and full of
undesirables but M'Conachie
told him you got a decent
enough do in the Brazen Head
over in Winetavern street
(which was distantly suggestive
to the person addressed of
friar Bacon) for a bob.*

8 The Ormond Hotel, 7–13 Ormond Quay

Crossing over the Father Mathew Bridge to the north quays, this riverside hotel is the setting for the 'Sirens' episode of *Ulysses*. Leopold Bloom has spied Blazes Boylan inside and enters as Boylan is setting to depart for his rendezvous with Molly.

The episode is one of the most challenging but beautiful in the book, taking as its form and subject music and song. Opening with a jumbled assortment of phrases that will recur throughout the episode (what Joyce described as a *fuga per canonem*), it delights in juxtaposing homonymic phrases, syllables and musical allusions in a manner that appropriates the mysterious sweep and sway of song.

What, Ormond? Best value in Dublin. Is that so?

John Joyce is said to have drunk regularly at the Ormond in the aftermath of his wife May's death, returning home to St. Peter's Terrace only to shout at and scold his daughters. The Ormond Hotel itself fell into disrepair after it closed in 2006. In the past few years there have been campaigns to both demolish and restore the building, but thanks to its cultural significance, it has repeatedly been saved from demolition.

9 Barney Kiernan's, Little Britain St.

Around the corner you can visit the site of another significant, albeit long closed, pub from *Ulysses*. The original pub was located just beside its current incarnation, in numbers 8 to 10.

This is the setting for the 'Cyclops' episode, where Bloom comes to meet Martin Cunningham. This episode is narrated by an unnamed man, who recounts Bloom's earlier run-in with the Citizen. Bloom refused to have a drink or buy a round, much to the dissatisfaction of everyone else in the pub, which provoked the anti-Semitic ire of the Citizen. The resulting confrontation eventually finds Bloom on the receiving end of a launched biscuit tin!

Set as it is in a dusty 'regular', the episode contains many wonderful allusions to the love of a good pint, such as this gem from the mouth of our unnamed narrator:

Ah! Owl! Don't be talking! I was blue mouldy for the want of that pint. Declare to God I could hear it hit the pit of my stomach with a click.

Now that you're thirsty – and you've reached the end of our James Joyce trails – why don't you pop around the corner to Capel Street to grab a quick scoop at one of the many fine establishments there?

Dedication

Mark: To Jen and Elsie, and in memory of my father, Leo.

Emily: To my father, who'll get the biggest kick out of this.

Acknowledgements

We must first offer our sincere thanks to Michael O'Brien for sticking with and supporting a book that was pitched to him quite casually some years ago. His encouragement and determination fostered the development of this little book. Thanks too goes to our editor, Nicola Reddy, whose skill and experience gave shape to the work, and who applied pressure and reassurance at all the right moments. And for all of the gang at O'Brien Press, who are a pleasure to work with – thank you!

We are grateful to our colleagues in the James Joyce Centre, as well as to all of those Joyceans who pass through its doors, and who have provided much insight both by way of their own books and through conversations. In particular we would like to thank Terence Killeen for casting his expert eye over the text and for imparting his knowledge at vital points in the writing process. Of course, any errors fall squarely at our feet.

Finally, we would like to acknowledge the support of our families: to the Carsons – Jean, Paul and David, and Yann Chalmers; to the Traynors – Jen, Elsie, Yvonne, Ross, Fiona and Anne Gibney; and to the O'Caseys and MacArees – Gay, Brian and Fin.